Nita Mehta

DIWALI COOKBOOK

Nita Mehta™
B.Sc. (Home Science), M.Sc. (Food and Nutrition), Gold Medalist

Introduction

If there is any festival to which India is associated with, globally, it is Diwali. Irrespective of colour, caste or creed this festival brings everyone together. Every home is illuminated and the week is filled with celebration and gusto.

Why not make this Diwali a very special one by following the detailed yet simple recipes given in this book? From dips and starters to main course followed by exquisite desserts – the book has them all.

Most of these recipes would be known to the readers, and yet each of them has something very special about it, enhancing the aroma, flarvour and good looks!

Go ahead and have a wonderful Diwali, this year and many more to come. Offer a feast to your loved ones with the help of this book which gives you the finesse in cooking.

Snab Publishers Pvt Ltd

Corporate Office
3A/3, Asaf Ali Road, New Delhi 110 002
Phone: +91 11 2325 2948, 2325 0091
E-mail: nitamehta@nitamehta.com
Website: www.nitamehta.com

ISBN 978-81-7869-465-8

Revised Edition 2014

Printed in India at Infinity Advertising Services (P) Ltd, New Delhi

Contributing Writers:
Anurag Mehta
Tanya Mehta
Subhash Mehta

Editors :
Sangeeta
Sunita

Distributed by :
NITA MEHTA BOOKS
3A/3, Asaf Ali Road, New Delhi - 02

Distribution Centre :
D16/1, Okhla Industrial Area, Phase-I,
New Delhi - 110020
Tel.: 26813199, 26813200
E-mail: nitamehta.mehta@gmail.com

Editorial and Marketing office
E-159, Greater Kailash II, New Delhi 110 048

Food Styling and Photography by Snab
Typesetting by National Information Technology Academy
3A/3, Asaf Ali Road, New Delhi 110 002

Recipe Development & Testing:
Nita Mehta Creative Arts - R & D Centre
3A/3, Asaf Ali Road, New Delhi - 110 002

Nita Mehta CREATIVE ARTS Creating Food Artists, not just chefs...

Price: Rs. 125/-

Contents

Snacks & Dips 5

Main Dishes 18

Mithai & Sweet Dishes 39

5-Day Celebrations

1st day
DHAN-TERAS

Buying a new utensil on this day is a tradition related to Dhanvantari Triyodashi.

2nd day
CHHOTI DIWALI

The second day of Diwali is Nark Chaturdashi. Legend has it that Lord Krishna killed the demon Narkasur on this day to make mankind free from his fear. It is a tradition to massage the body with oil and bathe on this day. It is believed that those who do not bathe on this day, go to *Nark* or hell!!

3rd day
BADI DIWALI or LAKSHMI PUJAN

Badi Diwali or Lakshmi Pujan is the main day of celebrations of the festival of Diwali. People perform Lakshmi Pujan on this day to be blessed with wealth and prosperity. They clean their homes and decorate it with lights and fire crackers.

4th Day
GOVARDHAN PUJA

The fourth day of Diwali is Govardhan Puja and, as the name itself suggests, is the worship of Govardhan Parvat. Kadhi chawal are made in most of the Hindu homes and offered the deities.

5th Day
BHAI DOOJ

Bhai Dooj, the fifth day, to celebrate the brother-sister relationship. Sisters put a tikka on their forehead and offer a variety of sweets to their brothers.

Snacks
&
Dips

Rani Seekh

Makes 20 pieces

INGREDIENTS

1 cup whole red lentils (*sabut masoor ki dal*)
1" piece of ginger - grated (1 tbsp)
10-12 flakes garlic - roughly chopped
2 green chillies - chopped
1 tsp cumin seeds (*jeera*)
½ capsicum - chopped finely
1 small onion - chopped
1 small tomato - chopped without pulp
1 cup roughly crumbled *paneer*
1 slice of bread - churned in a mixer to get fresh crumbs
4 tbsp cornflour
a pinch of cinnamon (*dalchini*) powder
¼ tsp green cardamom (*chhoti elaichi*) powder
1½ tsp salt, 2 tsp garam masala
1½ tsp red chilli powder
1 tsp dry mango powder (*amchoor*)
2 tsp lemon juice
7 tbsp oil

1. Soak dal for 2 hours in 3-4 cups water. Strain.
2. Grind dal, ginger, garlic, green chillies & cumin seeds in a mixer to a paste.
3. Heat 4 tbsp oil in a pan and add the dal paste, stir for 4-5 minutes. When the dal turns dry, remove from fire.
4. Add paneer, bread, cornflour, cinnamon powder, cardamom powder, salt, garam masala, red chilli, amchoor and lemon juice. Mash well with hands.
5. Add capsicum, onion & tomato. Mix well.
6. Shape the mixture into 2" long seekh kebabs.
7. Heat 3 tbsp oil in a pan and pan fry 4-5 kebabs at a time till golden brown from all sides. Add more oil, if required, for frying. Serve with chutney.

Smoked Mushroom Galouti Kebabs

Makes 8

INGREDIENTS

200 gm mushrooms, juice of 1 lemon
1 medium potato - boiled mashed
75 gms paneer - grated
2 tbsp ghee/oil
1 onion - chopped finely
1 tbsp finely chopped ginger
2 green chillies - chopped finely
½ tsp turmeric (*haldi*), ½ tsp red chilli powder
1 tbsp chopped coriander leaves
½ tsp salt, or to taste, ½ tsp garam masala

SMOKING

2" piece of charcoal (take a piece from your press waala)

GARNISH

lemon slices, onion rings, mint leaves
chaat masala to sprinkle

1. Boil 3 cups water with 1 tsp salt and juice of lemon. Add mushrooms and boil for 3-4 minutes. Strain. Chop finely. Keep aside.
2. Heat ghee or oil in a *kadhai*, add onions and saute till brown. Add ginger and green chillies, turmeric and chilli powder. Stir for a few seconds. Add the mushrooms, mashed potatoes and paneer. Mix well and remove from heat.
3. Add green coriander, salt and garam masala. Mash well with a potato masher or a *kadchhi*.
4. Place the mixture in a bowl. Place a small steel vessel (*katori*) in the center of the bowl. Hold the charcoal with a long tongs (*chimta*) and place it on fire. When it starts burning, place the live charcoal in the *katori*, pour 1 tsp ghee on the charcoal and immediately cover the bowl. Leave to smoke the mixture for 5 minutes.
5. Make round kebabs of the smoked mixture.
6. Heat a non stick pan or a tawa, grease with ½ tsp oil. Cook kebabs on medium heat till brown. Garnish with lemon slices, onion rings, mint leaves. Sprinkle chaat masala.

Dal ke Mini Samose

Makes 12

INGREDIENTS

COVERING

2 cups of flour (*maida*)

1½ tsp salt, 8 tbsp oil

FILLING

½ cup split moong beans (*dhuli moong dal*) - soak in 1 cup water overnight with

¼ tsp baking soda (*meetha soda*)

1 tsp cumin seeds (*jeera*)

1-2 pinches of asafoetida (*hing*) powder

1 tsp salt

1 tsp garam masala

1 tsp coriander (*dhania*) powder

½ tsp red chilli powder

½ tsp dry mango powder (*amchoor*)

5 tbsp oil, oil for frying

1. For the filling, strain dal. Roughly grind the moong dal in a mixer.
2. Heat 5 tbsp oil in a pan. Add cumin seeds and asafoetida powder. Cook till cumin seeds turns golden.
3. Add dal paste. Stir for 2-3 minutes. Add salt, garam masala, coriander powder, chilli powder and dry mango powder. Cook for 2-3 minutes on slow fire until the mixture dries up well. Remove from fire and keep aside.
4. For the covering, sieve flour and salt together. Add oil and mix it very well. Add ½ cup water and make a firm dough. Knead well to get a smooth dough. Make 6 small round balls of the dough.
5. Roll each ball into 4"-5" diameter chapatti. Cut it into 2 equal halves.
6. Put some water along the straight edge of the semi circle.
7. Join and press together to make a cone. Place a tbsp of filling in the cone and press to close the samosa. Make 12 samosas.
8. Heat oil in a kadhai and deep fry 6 pieces at a time on low medium heat till golden. Do not fry on high heat or the samosas will remain uncooked.
9. Drain on paper napkins. Serve hot with green chutney.

Aloo Channa Chaat

Serves 6

INGREDIENTS

2 medium sized potatoes - boiled, peeled and cut into 1" pieces
1 cup chick-peas (*kabuli channe*) - soaked overnight in water
2 tbsp mango chutney, ready-made or homemade
¾ tsp red chilli powder or to taste
1 tsp roasted cumin (*bhuna jeera*) powder
1 tsp chaat masala
2 green chillies - deseeded & finely chopped
4 tbsp chopped coriander leaves
1 small onion - finely chopped
1 tomato - deseeded and chopped
juice of 1 lemon
¼-½ tsp salt or to taste

1. Drain channe and pressure cook them in 3 cups water. Give 1 whistle, reduce heat to medium and cook for 7-8 minutes. Remove from fire. Let the pressure drop by itself. Strain channe.
2. Transfer to a bowl. Whisk the chutney and add to the channas. Mix well. Add all the remaining ingredients. Mix well. Taste and adjust the seasoning. Serve.

Masala Cashews

Serves 6

INGREDIENTS

250 gm large cashew nuts (*kaju*) - use whole or split into two pieces
½ tsp salt, ½ tsp red chilli powder
½ tsp garam masala
¼ tsp black pepper
a pinch of powdered citric acid or *amchoor*
a pinch of sugar
1½ tbsp ghee

1. Heat ghee in a large frying pan. Reduce heat. Add cashews. Fry stirring continuously till light golden, on low flame. Remove pan from fire.
2. Sprinkle all other ingredients over hot cashew nuts in the pan. Toss till masalas lightly coat the nuts. Remove from pan to a plate.
3. Cool completely to room temperature before storing in an airtight container.

Paneer Bites with Peanut Dip

Makes 24

INGREDIENTS

200 gm paneer, preferably packet paneer
200 gm small mushrooms - cut stalk completely and cut into 2 pieces

MARINADE

½ tsp salt, ½ tsp degi mirch
1 tsp brown sugar or gur
2 tbsp coconut milk, ready made
½ tsp soya sauce
½" piece of ginger - grated (1 tsp)
1 tsp lemon juice
1 tbsp cornflour
4 flakes garlic - crushed to a paste (1 tsp)
½ tsp ground cumin (*jeera*) powder
½ tsp coriander (*dhania*) powder

PEANUT DIP

¼ cup roasted salted peanuts
½ tsp salt
4-6 flakes garlic - crushed (1 tsp)
½ onion - chopped finely
½ tsp red chilli powder
1 tsp coriander (*dhania*) powder
1 tsp cumin (*jeera*) powder
¾ cup ready-made coconut milk
½ tsp sugar
1 tsp soya sauce
1½ tsp lemon juice
1 tbsp oil
a pinch of red chilli powder

1. Boil 3 cups water, add mushrooms in it. Boil for 2-3 minutes. Remove from fire, strain and refresh in cold water. Cut paneer into ½" thick slices. Cut each slice into 4 triangles.
2. Mix all ingredients of marinade together in a flat dish.
3. Thread a mushroom onto tooth picks, keeping it flat. Pierce a paneer piece and put the ready picks in the marinade in the flat dish (not bowl). Turn each tooth pick gently to coat. Cover and keep aside till serving time.
4. To make peanut dip, grind peanuts with the salt to a rough powder. Heat 1 tbsp oil in a heavy bottomed small pan or kadhai. Add crushed garlic. Stir. Add onion and cook till soft. Reduce heat. Add ½ tsp red chilli powder, coriander powder and cumin powder. Add only ½ cup coconut milk. Boil, stirring. Cook on low heat for 3 minutes, stirring constantly. Add crushed peanuts, ½ tsp sugar, 1 tsp soya sauce and remaining coconut milk. Boil. Simmer gently for 2 minutes, stirring occasionally to prevent it from sticking to the pan. Remove from fire. Add 1½ tsp lemon juice. Check taste for salt, sugar and lemon juice.
5. For tempering the dip, heat 1 tbsp oil. Remove from fire and add red chilli powder. Mix and pour over the peanut dip. Mix gently.
6. To serve paneer bites, heat 2 tbsp oil in a non-stick pan. Put the skewers on it. When the underside gets done turn the side. Do not turn till you get a nice brown colour. Brown the other side also. Serve with peanut dip.

Peshawari Broccoli Tikka

Serves 6

INGREDIENTS

500 gm (2 medium heads) broccoli - cut into medium sized florets with long stalks
2 tsp salt, 1 tsp sugar

1ST MARINADE

juice of 1 lemon (3-4 tsp)
½ tsp carom seeds (*ajwain*)
1 tsp salt and ½ tsp red chilli powder

2ND MARINADE

¾ cup thick yogurt - hang for one hour
2 tbsp grated cheese, 2 tbsp oil
4 tbsp cream or fresh malai
2 tbsp roasted cashews - grind with a little water to a paste
1 tbsp cornflour
2 tsp ginger-garlic paste
½ tsp red chilli paste, optional
½ tsp salt, ½ tsp garam masala
1 clove (*laung*) - crushed
seeds of 2 green cardamoms - crushed

1. Boil 5-6 cups of water in a large pan. Add 2 tsp salt and 1 tsp sugar to the water. Add broccoli pieces to the boiling water. Boil. Keep on boiling for a minute. Remove from heat and let broccoli be in hot water for 2 minutes. Drain. Refresh with cold water. Strain. Wipe the pieces well with a clean kitchen towel till well dried.
2. Spread the broccoli on a flat plate and sprinkle the ingredients of the 1st marinade. Mix well. Marinate the broccoli for 15 minutes.
3. For the 2nd marinade, mix cheese and oil till well blended. Add remaining ingredients and mix well. Pick up the broccoli pieces, leaving the water behind, and add to the yogurt marinade and mix well. Check salt. Refrigerate till the time of serving.
4. To serve, brush the grill rack of the oven or tandoor with some oil. Place the broccoli pieces on it and cook in a preheated oven at 210°C/410°F only for 10 minutes. Do not over cook it, it turns too dry. Serve hot.

Vadi Kebabs

Makes 15 pieces

INGREDIENTS

250 gms moong dal vadi
2 tbsp lemon juice
4 tbsp oil
¾ cup dry bread crumbs - enough to bind
¼ cup chopped coriander
red chilli powder and garam masala to taste

CRUSH TOGETHER

seeds of 4 green cardamoms (*chhoti elaichi*)
2 cloves (*laung*)

OTHER INGREDIENTS

¾ cup grated paneer
1½ tsp ginger-garlic paste
½ onion - finely chopped
3-4 green chillies - finely chopped
½ tomato - finely chopped
½ of a green capsicum
1 tsp salt or to taste

1. Boil vadi for 3-4 minutes in water. Pat dry on a kitchen towel. Cool. Break into pieces.
2. Grind vadi with all the other ingredients - paneer, ginger garlic, onion, coriander, chillies, tomato and capsicum. Add salt to taste.
3. Remove from grinder and add bread crumbs, lemon juice and 4 tbsp oil, coriander and freshly crushed spices. If the vadis are not spicy, add garam masala and red chilli powder to the kebab mixture.
4. Make small balls and flatten to make kebabs. Cook on a hot pan greased with just 2 tbsp oil till well browned on both sides. Serve hot.

Corn & Paneer Chaat

Serves 2-3

INGREDIENTS

1 cup frozen corn kernels, see note
1 tbsp softened butter
1 onion - chopped finely, 1 tomato - chopped
1 tbsp finely chopped coriander
1-2 green chillies - chooped
50 gms paneer - cut into tiny cubes
½ tsp black salt, ½ tsp chaat masala
½ tsp black pepper, salt to taste
1 tsp lemon juice, or to taste

Note: *you can boil fresh corn kernels also.*

1. Put corns in 1 cup water and microwave for 2-3 minutes. Alternately, put corns in boiling water for a minute. Strain corn kernels and put in a bowl. Mix butter with the hot corn.
2. Add all the other ingredients along with paneer and mix. Garnish with coriander leaves.

Namak Paare

Serves 4

INGREDIENTS

1 cup wheat flour (*atta*)
½ cup plain flour (*maida*)
6 tbsp oil, 1 tsp salt
¼ tsp carom seeds (*ajwain*), oil for frying

1. Sift both flours together.
2. Add oil, salt and carom seeds and mix well. Make a well in the center, add about ½ cup water gradually and knead into a stiff dough.
3. Roll out the dough into big round sized chappati, about ¼" thick. Cut it into ½" broad fingers with a knife.
4. Heat oil in a kadhai. Now put these long strips into the oil. Fry in 2-3 batches on low heat. Let the namak paare be in oil for 7-8 minutes till they get cooked properly and turn golden in colour.
5. Remove from oil. Drain on paper and serve. To store - spread out paare under the fan to cool down completely and keep in an airtight container.

Cheese Dip

Makes 1 small bowl

INGREDIENTS

1 cup yogurt - hang in a muslin cloth for 2-3 hours
2 tbsp cheese spread, ½ cup fresh cream
1 onion - chopped very fine
1 capsicum - deseeded & chopped fine
juice of ½ lemon, or to taste
salt and white pepper to taste

1. Beat the curd and cheese spread with a baloon whisk till smooth.
2. Mix cream gently.
3. Add all other ingredients & mix lightly. Chill. Serve in a small bowl with starters.

Smoked Red Pepper Dip

Makes 1 small bowl

INGREDIENTS

1 red bell pepper (red capsicum)
1 dry red chilli - soaked in water & microwave for 1 minute
1 flake garlic - finely chopped
½ tsp salt, ¼ tsp paprika
1 tsp cheese spread, ½ tsp lemon juice
1/3 cup extra virgin olive oil
a pinch of red chilli flakes
a pinch of fresh or dry parsley or oregano

1. Roast a washed red bell pepper on a naked flame for about 5 minutes till nicely black all over. Immediately put in a bowl and cover the bowl for 10 minutes for the pepper to sweat and acquire a nice smoky flavour. Peel the black skin. Wash your hands and peel again nicely but do not wash the pepper. Deseed the pepper and chop roughly. Keep aside.
2. In a small spice grinder, put drained and softened dry red chilli cut into bits, garlic, salt and paprika. Grind to a rough paste.
3. To the grinder add - chopped roasted pepper and grind again till smooth.
4. Add 1 tsp cheese spread, ½ tsp lemon juice and 1/3 cup olive oil to the red pepper in the grinder and grind again for a few seconds.
5. Add red chilli flakes & parsley or oregano. Remove to a small micro proof serving bowl. To serve, warm in a microwave for 30 seconds.
6. Serve as a dip with nachos, pizza crackers or with vegetable crudites.

Main
Dishes

Nilgiri Curry

Serves 4

INGREDIENTS

1 small potato - cut into fingers
4-6 medium cauliflower florets
5-6 French beans - sliced diagonally into 1" pieces
1 carrot - cut into 1" round slices
1 capsicum - cut into 1" pieces
5 tbsp oil, 2 onions - chopped
10-12 curry leaves
3 tomatoes - pureed in a mixer
1½ tsp salt or to taste
¼ cup chopped coriander leaves
¾ tsp garam masala powder
2-3 tbsp cream

MASALA PASTE

1 tsp chopped ginger, 1 tsp chopped garlic
1 tsp cumin seeds (*jeera*)
2 tbsp poppy seeds (*khus khus*)
5 cloves (*laung*)
2-3 dry red chillies, ½ cup grated coconut
2 tbsp coriander seeds (*sabut dhania*)
1 tbsp fennel seeds (*saunf*)

1. Heat 2 tbsp oil and add all ingredients of the masala paste, fry for 3-4 minutes. Remove from fire. Cool and grind to a paste with ¼ cup water.
2. Boil 3 cups water with ½ tsp salt and ½ tsp sugar in a saucepan. Add potatoes. Cook till done. Add cauliflower, beans and carrots. Give one boil. Remove from fire. Let veggies be in hot water for 2 minutes. Strain, reserving the boiled water. Keep aside.
3. Heat 3 tbsp oil in a kadhai, add onion and fry till golden brown.
4. Add curry leaves & the freshly prepared masala paste. Stir fry for 3-4 minutes.
5. Add tomato puree and bring to boil. Cook for 4-5 minutes on low heat.
6. Add salt, capsicum & blanched vegetables. Cook stirring for 2-3 minutes.
7. Add 1½ cups reserved boiled water from the vegetables and give one boil. Simmer for 3-4 minutes. Remove from fire. Add chopped coriander leaves and cream.
8. Sprinkle garam masala, stir well. Serve hot with boiled rice or roti.

Pudina Paneer

Serves 4

INGREDIENTS

250 gm paneer - cut into 1" triangular or square pieces
3 big onions - sliced
½ tsp turmeric (*haldi*) powder
1 tsp red chilli powder
¾ tsp salt
2 big tomatoes - cut each tomato into 4 pieces lengthwise, remove pulp, chop the pulp and cut the outer skin into 1" pieces
2 tbsp dry pudina powder (read tip, given below)
1 tsp garam masala
4 tbsp oil

1. Heat 4 tbsp oil and add sliced onions, cook till brown.
2. Add turmeric, red chilli powder & salt.
3. Add pulp of tomatoes and cook for 4-5 minutes or till dry.
4. Add paneer, dried mint, tomato pieces and garam masala. Cook for 2 minutes and remove from fire. Serve hot.

TIP: *Drying pudina in a microwave ...*

Spread 1 cup pudina leaves in a flat micro-proof plate. Microwave for 2 minutes. Give standing time for 2 minutes. Remove from microwave and leave it outside for 2 hours till dry. Store in an air tight bottle. To use, crush with the hands roughly.

Makai Mirch

Makes 10

INGREDIENTS

10 big, thick dark green chillies with stem (250 gms)

MARINADE

3 tbsp lemon juice, 3 tbsp white vinegar
½ tsp garlic paste
½ tsp salt, ¼ tsp pepper, ½ tsp sugar

STUFFING

½ tin cream style sweet corn (1 cup)
2 tbsp oil, 1 onion - chopped finely
½ tsp crushed garlic
½ tsp chopped ginger
1 tsp tomato ketchup
½ tsp salt, ¼ tsp pepper
1 tsp white vinegar
1 cheese cube - diced into tiny pieces

1. Cut a slit lengthwise in each chilli, leaving the edges intact to hold the filling well. Scoop out the seeds with the help of a knife.
2. Mix all the ingredients of the marinade in a bowl. Put 1 tbsp of marinade in each chilli slit, shake it well and remove the marinade to the bowl to reuse it. Similarly do with all chillies. Leave aside for ½ hour.
3. For the stuffing, heat oil in a pan. Add onion and cook till it turns golden.
4. Add garlic and ginger. Stir for a few seconds.
5. Add cream style corn. Cook for 1-2 minutes.
6. Add ketchup, salt, pepper and vinegar. Cook for 2-3 minutes till dry.
7. Stuff the chillies with this filling. They should be stuffed well but not to bursting point. Cover with a wrap and refrigerate till serving time.
8. To serve, cook in a pan with 2-3 tbsp oil. Keep the chillies spread out while cooking. Turn when it turns brownish from the bottom. When both sides get lightly browned, cover and cook on low heat for 3-4 minutes till soft.

Haryali Kofta Curry

Serves 6-8

INGREDIENTS

1 large bunch (800 gm) spinach - discard stalks and roughly chop the leaves
1 green chilli - chopped
3 tbsp ghee or oil, 1 onion - chopped
1 tsp garlic paste
1 tsp finely chopped ginger
¾ tsp garam masala, ½ tsp red chilli powder
1¼ tsp salt or to taste
2 tomatoes - puree in a mixer
seeds of 1 green cardamom (*chhoti elaichi*) - powdered
1 cup milk, ½ cup cream, optional

15 KOFTAS

3 potatoes - boiled, peeled and grated finely
2 slices bread - churned in a mixer to get fresh crumbs
½ small onion - very finely chopped
¾ cup boiled peas - mashed roughly
1 tsp chopped green chilli
1 tbsp chopped coriander
¼ tsp garam masala
5-6 almonds - chopped
¼ tsp dry mango powder (*amchoor*)
1¼ tsp salt, oil for frying

1. Clean and wash spinach. Cook covered for 5-6 minutes in a kadhai with ¼ cup water on low heat till spinach turns soft. Do not open in between. Remove from fire and let it cool down covered for 5 minutes. After it cools down, drain the water to remove the bitterness. Add ¾ cup fresh water and grind spinach to a smooth paste in a mixer with 1 green chilli.
2. Heat 3 tbsp ghee or oil in a pan, add chopped onion and ginger. Saute for a few minutes till golden. Add garlic. Stir for a few seconds. Add garam masala powder, chilli powder and salt. Add pureed tomatoes and cardamom powder. Cook till oil separates for about 5-6 minutes.
3. Add ground spinach, cook uncovered for 5-7 minutes on medium flame.
4. Add milk. Mix well & cook for 2 minutes. Remove from fire. Add cream.
5. For koftas, mix all the ingredients. Add 1-2 tbsp water if the koftas do not bind together. Divide mixture into equal portions and shape into balls. Deep fry 1-2 koftas at a time in hot oil till golden brown in colour.
6. To serve place the gravy in a serving bowl. Arrange koftas over it. Microwave to heat through.

Chana Mushroom Mix

Serves 4

INGREDIENTS

1 cup chick-peas (*kabuli channa*) - soaked overnight
200 gm mushrooms - cut into thick slices
2 big onions - chopped
1 tbsp finely chopped garlic
1 tsp chopped ginger
2 green chillies - remove seeds and slit lengthwise, 3 tsp curry powder
1 tsp cumin (*jeera*) powder
1 tbsp channa masala
1¼ tsp salt, 1 tsp garam masala
4 tbsp oil

1. Drain the soaked channas. Pressure cook channas with 4 cups water to give 3 whistles. Reduce heat and cook for 15 minutes. Remove from fire. Let the pressure drop by itself.
2. To blanch mushrooms, boil 2-3 cups of water with 1 tbsp lemon juice and 1 tsp salt in a saucepan, add sliced mushrooms, boil for 1 minute. Strain.
3. Heat oil in a kadhai, add onions, garlic, ginger and chilli. Cook for about 5 minutes.
4. Add curry powder and cumin powder. Stir well.
5. Add mushrooms, chick-peas, chana masala & salt. Stir fry for 4-5 minutes.
6. Add 1 cup water and cook on slow fire for 10-12 minutes.
7. Add garam masala powder, stir and remove from heat. Serve hot.

Khatti Dal

Serves 4

INGREDIENTS

½ cup split yellow lentils (*arhar* or *tur dal*)
3 tbsp oil or ghee
½ tsp black mustard seeds (*sarson*)
½ tsp cumin (*jeera*)
a few curry leaves, 2 red/green chillies
3 cloves (*laung*)
1 bay leaf (*tej patta*),
¼ tsp coriander (*dhania*) powder
½ tsp turmeric (*haldi*)
1 walnut size ball of imli - soaked in ½ cup water, boiled & strained to get ¼ cup imli pulp
1 tsp black Maharashtrian masala or channa masala
1½ tsp salt, or to taste
1 tbsp finely chopped coriander
¼ tsp garam masala

1. Wash and soak dal for 15 minutes.
2. Pressure cook dal with 3 cups of water to give 4 whistles. Keep for 10 minutes on medium fire till very soft. Remove from fire. Let the pressure drop by itself.
3. Mash dal slightly.
4. Heat 3 tbsp oil or ghee in a clean kadhai. Add mustard seeds, cumin and and curry leaves. Allow them to splutter. Add chillies, cloves, bay leaf, and coriander powder, saute for one minute. Add turmeric. Stir.
5. Add ¼ cup imli pulp and fry further for one minute.
6. Add dal. Add maharashtran masala or channa masala and salt.
7. Bring to a boil and simmer dal for 8-10 minutes. Add chopped coriander and garam masala. Serve hot.

Bhindi Masala

Serves 4-5

INGREDIENTS

400 gm lady's finger (*bhindi*) - small & tender
3 tbsp oil
½ tsp turmeric (*haldi*) powder
1¼ tsp salt, ¼ tsp red chilli powder
¼ tsp garam masala
1 tsp coriander (*dhania*) powder
½ tsp dry mango powder (*amchoor*)
2-3 green chillies - slit lengthwise on one side, keeping them whole

MASALA

2 tbsp oil, ½ tsp carom seeds (*ajwain*)
2 onions - sliced finely
1 tsp chopped ginger
4-6 flakes of garlic - crushed to a paste (1 tbsp)
½ tsp salt, 2 tsp coriander powder
½ tsp red chilli powder
¼ tsp turmeric (*haldi*) powder
1 tsp ground cumin (*jeera*) powder
2 tomatoes - chopped
4 tbsp ready made tomato puree
1-2 tbsp coriander - finely chopped
2 cloves (*laung*) and seeds of 2 green cardamoms - crushed together
½ tsp garam masala
½ tsp chaat masala

1. Wash, drain bhindi. Wipe dry with a clean kitchen towel. (The lady's finger should not be wet). Slice off ¼" from the head of each lady's finger. Make a slit in each piece, keeping the lady's finger whole.
2. Heat 3 tbsp oil in a kadhai or a non stick wok. Add turmeric. Mix well. Add lady's finger. Cook without covering keeping the lady's finger spread out in the kadhai for 5-7 minutes. Cover and cook for 5-7 minutes, on slow flame stirring occasionally, till almost done. If you like, you can deep fry the bhindi.
3. Sprinkle salt, and all other masalas. Add whole green chillies. Cook uncovered on a slow fire, stirring occasionally, till cooked. Keep aside.
4. For the masala, heat 2 tbsp oil, add carom seeds. Wait for 1 minute. Add onions. Stir fry till golden brown. Add ginger and garlic. Stir for a minute. Add salt, coriander powder, red chilli powder, turmeric & cumin powder. Stir.
5. Add tomatoes and tomato puree. Cook for about 5-7 minutes on medium flame till oil separates.
6. Add powdered cloves and green cardamoms. Add fresh coriander. Mix well.
7. Add the cooked bhindi to the masala. Add garam masala and chaat masala. Mix well. Check salt and add if needed. Serve hot.

TIP: *To keep the cooked bhindi crisp, add salt almost at the end. If added earlier, the bhindi turns soft.*

Tarka Beans

Serves 4

INGREDIENTS

250 gm french beans - cut into 2" long pieces
3 tbsp oil, ½ tsp mustard seeds (*rai*)
1 onion - chopped finely
¼ tsp turmeric (*haldi*), ¼ tsp salt
7-8 curry leaves
6-8 cashews (*kaju*) - soak in ¼ cup hot water for 10 minutes, grind to a smooth paste
½ tsp red chilli powder
2 tsp coriander (*dhania*) powder
½ tsp cumin seeds (*jeera*) powder
1 tbsp desiccated coconut
2 tbsp tomato puree, ready made
1 tsp garlic paste, ½ tsp ginger paste
¼ tsp garam masala
¼ tsp green cardamom powder

1. Heat oil. Add rai and curry leaves. Wait for 1 minute. Add ginger-garlic paste, stir for a few seconds. Add chopped onion and fry for 5 minutes till soft. Add french beans and saute for 5 minutes. Add ¼ cup water, turmeric and salt and cover and cook for 10-12 minutes on medium flame till beans get tender and a little water is left.
2. Add kaju paste, red chilli powder, cumin powder, coriander powder. Stir for 2-3 minutes on medium flame till dry. Add desiccated coconut and tomato puree. Cook for 1 minute. Add garam masala and cardamom powder. Serve.

Mughlai Phool Gobhi

Serves 4

INGREDIENTS

800 gm cauliflower (1 large *phool gobhi*) - cut into 2" florets
5 tbsp oil
1 tsp carom seeds (*ajwain*)
4 tbsp gram flour (*besan*)
4 tsp garlic paste (12-14 flakes of garlic)
½ cup ready-made tomato puree or ¾ cup fresh tomato puree
1 tsp salt
1 tsp red chilli powder
2 tsp cumin (*jeera*) powder
4 tbsp water
oil for deep frying
1 tsp garam masala
2 tbsp chopped coriander leaves (*hara dhania*)

GARNISH (OPTIONAL)

5 tbsp grated paneer

1. Heat oil for deep frying in a kadhai and deep fry the cauliflower florets till golden. Keep aside.
2. Heat 5 tbsp oil in a kadhai and add carom seeds. Stir for a second.
3. Add gram flour and fry for 1-2 minutes.
4. Add garlic paste and stir.
5. Add tomato puree and cook till oil separates for about 5 minutes.
6. Add salt, red chilli powder and cumin powder and water. Cook for 1-2 minutes. Keep aside till serving time.
7. At serving time, heat puree masala and add the fried cauliflower pieces, garam masala and coriander. Mix gently so as not to break the cauliflower pieces.
8. Serve in a flat serving dish and garnish with grated paneer if you like. Serve hot with roti or parantha.

Kadhai Baby Corns

Serves 4

INGREDIENTS

200 gm baby corns (20 pieces approx.)
juice of ½ lemon
2 small capsicums preferably 1 green and 1 red - cut into thin fingers
1-2 dry red chillies - deseeded
2 tsp coriander seeds (*sabut dhania*)
a pinch of fenugreek seeds (*methi daana*)
2 tsp ginger-garlic paste
2 onions - chopped
2 tomatoes - chopped
½ cup tomato puree
1 tbsp dry fenugreek leaves (*kasoori methi*)
¼ tsp turmeric (*haldi*)
½ tsp garam masala
1¼ tsp salt, or to taste
2 tbsp chopped coriander
½" piece ginger - cut into match sticks or shredded on the grater (1 tsp)
5 tbsp oil

1. Boil 4 cups water with 2 tsp salt and lemon juice. Add baby corns and boil for 2 minutes. Drain. Refresh in cold water. Cut into 2 pieces lengthwise, if thick.
2. Warm red chillies and coriander seeds on a tawa, till slightly crisp and dry, for about 30 seconds. Grind chillies and coriander seeds to a rough powder.
3. Heat 2 tbsp oil in a pan and add the boiled baby corns. Bhuno for 4-5 minutes till they start turning brown. Keep them spaced while bhunoing and do not overlap. Add the capsicum strips and stir fry for 2 minutes. Remove from kadhai and keep aside.
4. Heat 3 tbsp oil in a kadhai. Remove from fire. Add a pinch of fenugreek seeds, dhania-red chilli powder. Stir for 30 seconds.
5. Return to fire. Add onion. Cook till onions turn light golden. Add garlic-ginger paste. Mix well for a minute.
6. Add tomatoes and stir for about 4-5 minutes on low heat till dry. Add puree.
7. Add salt, fenugreek leaves, turmeric and garam masala. Add coriander. Mix well till oil separates. Add ½ cup water. Let it boil.
8. Add baby corns, capsicum and ginger. Cook for 2-3 minutes. Serve hot.

Khoye wale Shahi Gatte

Serves 4

INGREDIENTS

DOUGH

1¼ cups gram flour (*besan*)
a pinch of baking soda (*mitha soda*)
¾ tsp cumin seeds (*jeera*)
¼ tsp red chilli powder, ½ tsp salt
2 tsp chopped ginger
1 tbsp ghee, 2½ tbsp yogurt

FILLING

50 gms paneer
50 gms milk solids (*khoya*)
salt to taste
2 green chillies - finely chopped

CURRY

2 tbsp oil
1 tsp cumin seeds (*jeera*)
a pinch asafoetida (*hing*)
1 cup ready made tomato puree
1 cup yogurt - whisked well till smooth
4 tsp coriander powder
2 tsp red chilli powder
1 tsp turmeric (*haldi*) powder
½ tsp garam masala powder

1. Mix gram flour with all ingredients of the dough. Add some warm water to make a hard, but pliable dough. Knead well and keep aside covered.
2. For the filling, grate khoya and paneer. Mix grated khoya, paneer, chopped green chillies and a pinch of salt.
3. Divide dough into 3 portions. Roll out a portion to a 5" long oval shape and then place khoya paneer lengthwise in it. Carefully cover the stuffing with the dough on the sides and roll nicely to seal. Give it a cylindrical shape. Repeat this with the left over dough and filling.
4. Boil enough water in a medium deep pan so that the gatte can dip in water properly. Add ½ tsp salt. Add these stuffed gatte in boiling salted water. Boil for about 10 minutes. Remove from water when done. Keep water aside. Let them cool. Cut boiled gatte into 1" pieces. Deep fry and keep aside.
5. For preparing curry, heat oil, add cumin seeds, when they turn golden, add tomato puree, red chilli powder, asafoetida and turmeric powder, cook until oil starts separating.
6. Mix yogurt with coriander powder. Lower the heat and add yogurt, stirring continuously. Add 1 cup water of the gatte. Boil. Adjust salt, add garam masala powder. Add gatte and cook for 2-3 minutes until gravy thickens. Serve hot.

Vegetable Jalfrezi

Serves 4

INGREDIENTS

150 gms paneer - cut into small fingers
3 tbsp oil
½ tsp cumin seeds (*jeera*)
¼ tsp onion seeds (*kalaunji*)
15-20 curry leaves - roughly torn
1 onion - sliced
2 tsp ginger-garlic paste
8-10 French beans - sliced diagonally into 1" pieces or 8-10 babycorns - each halved lengthwise
1 large carrot - cut diagonally into thin slices
½ of each - green and yellow capsicum - deseed and cut into thin fingers
½ cup boiled peas
1 long, firm tomato - cut into 4, pulp removed and cut into thin long pieces
1 tsp dry fenugreek leaves (*kasoori methi*)

MIX TOGETHER

½ cup tomato puree, 1 tbsp tomato ketchup
½ tsp degi mirch powder, ½ tsp sugar
1 tsp coriander (*dhania*) powder
¼ tsp dried mango powder (*amchoor*)
1 tsp salt

1. Mix together — tomato puree, tomato ketchup, degi mirch powder, sugar, coriander powder, dry mango powder and salt in a cup. Keep aside.
2. Heat 3 tbsp oil in a kadhai. Add the cumin seeds and onion seeds together. When cumin turns golden, reduce heat and add curry leaves and stir for a few seconds.
3. Add onion & stir till golden. Add ginger-garlic and stir for a minute.
4. Add carrot and beans/babycorns. Saute for 2-3 minutes.
5. Add the tomato puree mixed with dry masalas, dry fenugreek leaves and stir on medium heat for 2 minutes.
6. Add ¼ cup water. Cook on low heat for about 4-5 minutes, till vegetables are cooked but still remain crunchy.
7. Add the capsicums, boiled peas, paneer and tomato slices. Stir for 1-2 minutes, till well blended. Add a pinch of sugar if needed. Remove from heat. Serve hot.

Khoya Makai

Serves 4-6

INGREDIENTS

200 gm baby corns
100 gm khoya - grated (½ cup)
3 tbsp ghee
1 tsp cumin (*jeera*)
1 tbsp finely chopped ginger
1 tbsp finely chopped green chillies
1 bay leaf (*tej patta*)
½ cup tomato puree, readmade
4 tomatoes - grated
2 tsp coriander powder
1 tsp salt, 1 tsp red chilli powder
½ tsp garam masala powder
1 tsp subzi masala, optional
½ tsp dry mango powder (*amchoor*)
½ tsp turmeric (*haldi*) powder
4 tbsp malai/cream
2 tbsp finely chopped coriander leaves

PASTE

2 tbsp poppy seeds (*khus khus*)
2 tbsp melon seeds (*magaz*)

1. Boil baby corns in 4 cups water with 1 tsp salt for 3-4 minutes. Strain and keep aside.
2. Soak poppy seeds and melon seeds in ½ cup hot water for 15 minutes. Drain and grind to a paste with a little water.
3. Heat ghee in a pan. Add cumin, bay leaf, ginger and green chillies. Stir for 2 minutes. Add the prepared paste and stir for a minute.
4. Add tomato puree, grated tomato, coriander powder, salt, red chilli powder, garam masala powder, subzi masala, dry mango powder and turmeric powder. Stir for 3-4 minutes.
5. Add baby corns & stir for 3-4 minutes.
6. Add khoya and bhuno for 2 minutes. Add malai and saute till ghee separates.
7. Add 1 cup water to get a masala gravy. Simmer for 2-3 minutes. Serve.

Subz Hyderabadi

Serves 6

INGREDIENTS

2 potatoes - cut into ¾" pieces
2 medium carrots - cut into ¼" thick slices
12-15 French beans - cut into 1½" pieces
10-12 medium florets of cauliflower
2 thin, long brinjals - cut into half lengthwise and then cut diagonally into 1½" pieces
¼ cup frozen or boiled peas
3 medium size onions - thinly sliced
1 tsp ginger paste
1 tsp garlic paste
1 tsp salt, ¼ tsp turmeric (*haldi*) powder
1 tsp red chilli powder
1 cup yogurt - whisked till very smooth
oil for frying

GRIND TOGETHER

seeds of 2 green cardamoms (*elaichi*)
4 cloves (*laung*)
1 bay leaf (*tej patta*)
¼" piece of cinnamon (*dalchini*)
¼ tsp black cumin seeds (*shah jeera*)

1. Heat oil in a kadhai for deep frying. Deep fry potatoes on low medium heat till golden and almost cooked. Remove from oil. Add cauliflower and fry till light golden, for about 2 minutes. Add brinjals and deep fry till they start changing colour. Add the carrots and fry for just a minute to retain their colour. Similarly fry the beans for just a minute. Set aside.
2. Remove excess oil from the kadhai, leaving about 4 tbsp oil. Heat oil and add onions. Fry for 8-10 minutes till golden brown.
3. Reduce heat. Add ginger and garlic and fry for a minute. Add salt, turmeric and red chilli powder. Sprinkle 2-3 tbsp water and simmer for 2-3 minutes for the spices to blend well.
4. Keeping the heat to a minimum, add the fried vegetables and whisked yogurt. Stir and cook at medium-low heat, till the vegetables are fully cooked. Sprinkle a little water while cooking, if required.
5. Add the ground spices and mix well. Serve hot.

Ranjit Masala Paneer

Serves 8-10

INGREDIENTS

500 gm paneer - cut into 1" pieces

MARINADE

2 tbsp ginger-garlic paste
½ tsp salt, ½ tsp red chilli powder
½ tsp lemon juice

MASALA

1 tbsp ghee
2 bay leaves (*tej patta*), 3-4 dry red chillies
4-5 green cardamoms (*elaichi*)
6-8 cloves (*laung*), 2-3 black peppercorns
1 tsp salt
8 large tomatoes (800 gm) - chopped
2 tbsp butter, 1 tsp cumin seeds (*jeera*)
3 onions - chopped
2 green chillies - chopped
2 tbsp chopped coriander leaves
15-20 almonds - ground to a powder
2 tbsp thick cream
1 tbsp dry fenugreek leaves (*kasoori methi*)

1. Crumble half of the paneer roughly, leaving half the paneer in pieces.
2. Marinate the paneer pieces with ginger-garlic paste, ½ tsp salt, lemon juice and red chilli powder. Keep aside.
3. Heat ghee in a kadhai, add bay leaves, 3-4 dry red chillies, 4-5 green cardamoms, 6-8 cloves and peppercorns. Stir for a minute till fragrant.
4. Add chopped tomatoes. Add 1 tsp of salt and cover and simmer on low heat for 3-4 minutes, till the tomatoes are slightly soft. Cool the mixture, blend in a mixer and sieve to get a smooth puree. Keep aside.
5. Heat butter in a clean kadhai, add cumin seeds, stir, and add chopped onions. Cook on medium heat till light brown. Add the chopped green chillies and coriander.
6. Stir for a minute, add the marinated paneer and cook for 1 minute. Add the tomato puree and mix well.
7. Add almond powder and stir to mix well. Add ½ cup water and boil for a minute. Add cream and cook for 1 minute. Add the crumbled paneer and fenugreek leaves. Mix and check the salt (if needed add more). Garnish with coriander leaves. Serve hot.

Mithai
&
Sweet
Dishes

Gulab ki Kheer

Serves 4-5

INGREDIENTS

1 litre full cream milk
4 tbsp tukda basmati rice - wash nicely
1½ cups fresh rose petals (*desi gulab*) - wash well
4 tbsp sugar, 4 tbsp water
1 tsp rose water or a few drops of rose essence, 1-2 tbsp rose syrup, optional

TIP: *Desi Gulab (rose) is preferred for this kheer. These petals are available easily at temples or with florists.*

1. Boil milk with rice in a heavy bottom deep kadhai. Cover and cook on medium heat for about 15-20 minutes till the rice is cooked. Uncover and cook for 15 minutes till you get the desired consistency. Remove from fire.
2. Boil 4 tbsp sugar with 4 tbsp water till you get a thick sugar syrup. Add rose petals and cook for 2-3 minutes. Remove from fire. Mix well. After it cools slightly, grind roughly in a mixer.
3. Add rose mix to the kheer and mix well. Add rose water. Check sweetness and add some powdered sugar or rose syrup if needed. Serve chilled.

Atta Besan Laddu

Makes 15 laddus

INGREDIENTS

2 cups whole wheat flour (*atta*)
1 cup gram flour (*besan*)
1 cup powdered sugar, preferably boora
¼ cup finely chopped mixed dry fruits (almonds, raisins, cashews etc.)
¾ cup ghee

1. Heat ghee in a kadhai. Add atta & gram flour. Roast on very low heat for about 15 minutes, stirring constantly, till the flour changes colour & gives out a fragrant roasted smell. Remove from fire.
2. Add finely chopped dry fruits in the mixture.
3. Add ground sugar and mix thoroughly. Make balls. Let them cool to room temperature. Store in an air tight box.

Pista Sandesh

Serves 6-8

INGREDIENTS

1 litre full cream milk (5 cups)
2 tbsp vinegar, 2 tbsp water
7 tbsp powdered sugar or to taste
1 tbsp cornflour
2 tbsp pistachio - grind to a powder
a few drops of green colour

GARNISH

a few whole pistachio pieces

1. Boil the milk. Mix vinegar in water and gradually add it to the milk till the milk curdles. Strain the chhena in a muslin cloth. Dip the chhena tied in the cloth in ice cold water for 10 minutes to stop further cooking. Hang the chhena in the cloth for 30 minutes to drain all water.
2. Grind chhena, sugar and cornflour in mixer till it is smooth. Transfer to a heavy bottomed kadhai.
3. Cook the chhena mixture for 8-10 minutes on low heat, keeping the chenna spread out on the sides of the kadhai to avoid getting too much heat. The paneer should not change colour. It should turn dry and become thick.
4. Remove to a bowl, add powdered pistachio and green colour. Make round and flattened pieces. Decorate with pistachio. Refrigerate till serving time.

Kesari Phirni

Serves 6

INGREDIENTS

3½ cups (700 gm) milk
1/3 cup basmati rice
1/3 cup sugar (slightly less than ½ cup) or to taste
25 almonds
5-6 green pistachios - soaked, peeled & sliced
2 small silver leaves - optional
seeds of 2-3 green cardamoms (*chhoti elaichi*) - powder
1 drop kewra essence or 1 tsp ruh kewra
a pinch of yellow colour

DECORATION

a few rose petals - dipped in cold water, a few strands kesar - soaked in warm water
a few fresh anaar ke daane

1. Soak rice of good quality for about 2-3 hours and then grind very fine with 4 to 5 tablespoonfuls of cold water to a paste. (You may soak rice overnight and keep in the fridge.)
2. Cut 5 almonds finely and keep aside. Boil remaining 20 almonds in water for 2-3 minutes. Peel, skin and grind to a paste with some water till smooth.
3. Dissolve the rice paste in ½ cup milk and make it thin.
4. Mix the rice paste with the remaining 3 cups milk in a heavy bottomed pan. Now keep on fire and cook on medium heat, stirring continuously, till the mixture is of creamy consistency, about 5 minutes.
5. Add the kesar water or a drop of colour, sugar and cardamom powder and stir. Simmer till sugar is fully dissolved and then boil for 5-6 minutes on medium heat.
6. Remove from fire. Add almond paste. Mix well.
7. Add ruh kewra or the essence and half of the shredded almonds and pistachios.
8. Pour the mixture into 6 small earthern containers. Chill. Decorate each dish with a silver leaf, rose petals, kesar and the remaining shredded nuts. Top with some fresh anaar ke daane if you like.

Meethe Chaawal

Serves 4

INGREDIENTS

1 cup Basmati rice - must be soaked for 1 hour
a pinch of yellow colour or saffron (*kesar*)
1 cup sugar
4 tbsp desi ghee
4 green cardamoms (*chhoti elaichi*)
3 cloves (*laung*)
8-10 cashews - halved
1 tbsp raisins (*kishmish*)
1 tbsp almonds (*badam*) - blanched & shredded

1. Mix ¾ cup water and 1 cup sugar in a small pan. Keep on fire to boil. Stir in between. Remove from fire as soon as syrup boils. Keep aside.
2. Heat ghee in a big heavy bottomed pan. Reduce heat. Add green cardamoms and cloves. Stir fry for a few seconds till cardamoms changes colour. Add cashews and stir till golden. Add almonds and raisins. Stir till raisins swells.
3. Discard water and add rice. Mix gently. Add 1½ cups water. Add colour or saffron. Boil.
4. Reduce flame as soon as the boil comes. Keep a tawa under the pan of rice as soon as it starts to boil to reduce the heat further. Cook for about 7-8 minutes till the water gets absorbed.
5. Add sugar syrup. Mix lightly with a fork. Cook further for 3-4 minutes till rice is done and dry. Shut off the flame but leave the rice in steam for 10 minutes. Fluff with a fork to serve.

Cream & Biscuit Pudding

Serves 8

INGREDIENTS

24 marie biscuits
400 gm thick cream - chilled (2 cups)
½ cup powdered sugar or to taste
½ tsp vanilla essence
3 tbsp chopped mixed nuts and raisins
¾ cup luke warm water mixed with ¼ cup powdered sugar
2½ tbsp cocoa powder

1. Add powdered sugar and essence to the cream.
2. Whip cream with an electric egg beater till it becomes thick and stiff. Mix in nuts and raisins. Keep aside.
3. Mix luke warm water and sugar together. Add cocoa powder and mix well.
4. Dip 3-4 biscuits at a time in the cocoa liquid.
5. Keep turning the biscuits with your fingers till the biscuits are a little soggy. Don't let them be too soggy.
6. Arrange a layer of these biscuits (about 10-12) in a flat glass dish.
7. Cover with a layer of whipped cream.
8. Arrange another layer of biscuits dipped in cocoa liquid on the cream. Spread the remaining cream as a thick layer on top.
9. Spoon 2-3 tbsp of the left over cocoa liquid on the top layer of cream, putting it randomly. Swirl lightly to get a marbled effect. Refrigerate for 4-5 hours before serving.

Gulab Jamun

Makes 16

INGREDIENTS

250 gm very smooth khoya (*dab khoya*)
5 tbsp plain flour (*maida*)
ghee for frying
2 cups sugar
3 cups water
1 green cardamom - crushed roughly
1 tsp green cardamom (*elaichi*) powder &
7-8 pistas - finely chopped

1. For balls, blend maida and khoya in a mixer for a few seconds. Remove from mixer and knead it properly with the palm on a flat surface till it no longer sticks to the surface. Knead to a soft dough.
2. For syrup, mix water, sugar & cardamom in a big saucepan. Bring to a boil and simmer for about 15-20 minutes till you get a 1 string syrup (ek taar ki chhanshi). Remove from fire.
3. Make balls from the dough. Flatten and put a pinch of cardamom powder and a pinch of pista in each ball. Form a ball again, taking care to remove all cracks.
4. Heat ghee for deep frying. Reduce heat. When the ghee is just slightly hot, add about 5 gulab jamuns and fry on very low flame for about 10 minutes till golden brown. Do not touch the balls too much, just shake the kadhai slightly or keep stirring the spoon in oil around the balls which keeps turning the balls. The balls will not increase in size while frying. Remove when done.
5. Add balls to the syrup, bring it to a good boil and switch off the gas. Keep balls in the syrup for about 30 minutes. The balls should absorb the liquid and swell in the syrup. They will float in the syrup. Serve hot.

Shahi Paneer Delight

Serves 8-10

INGREDIENTS

6 slices of bread - remove sides and cut each into 4 pieces, deep fry till golden brown
5 tbsp of chopped mixed nuts (almonds, raisins, pista etc.)
½ cup cold milk - to soak bread

PANEER LAYER

4 cups milk, ½ cup sugar
100 gms paneer - grated
¾ tsp powdered seeds of green cardamom
8 tsp cornflour dissolved in ½ cup milk
2 drops of kewra essence or ½ tsp kewra jal

1. For the paneer layer, boil 4 cups milk in a clean heavy bottomed kadhai. Simmer on low flame for 20 minutes.
2. Meanwhile, boil ½ cup sugar with ½ cup water in a separate pan. Keep on low heat for 5 minutes. Add grated paneer. Cook for 1 minute. Remove from fire.
3. Add cornflour paste to the thickened milk of step 1, stirring continuously. Keep boiling for 2 minutes till thick. Add sugar and paneer mixture. Boil. Keep on heat for 1 minute. Remove from fire. Cool. Add essence and half of the nuts. Sprinkle elaichi powder. Keep aside.
4. Dip a piece of fried bread in some cold milk for a second. Remove immediately.
5. Take a serving dish. Spread 1/3 of paneer mixture at the bottom of the dish.
6. Place 12 pieces of fried and soaked bread in a single layer at the base of the dish.
7. Spread about ½ of the paneer mixture on the bread.
8. Repeat the bread layer in the same way with bread pieces and then cover with the paneer layer. Top with nuts.
9. Cover with a cling wrap (plastic film) and let it set for at least 1 hour before serving. Serve at room temperature.

INTERNATIONAL CONVERSION GUIDE

These are not exact equivalents; they've been rounded-off to make measuring easier.

WEIGHTS & MEASURES

METRIC	*IMPERIAL*
15 g	½ oz
30 g	1 oz
60 g	2 oz
90 g	3 oz
125 g	4 oz (¼ lb)
155 g	5 oz
185 g	6 oz
220 g	7 oz
250 g	8 oz (½ lb)
280 g	9 oz
315 g	10 oz
345 g	11 oz
375 g	12 oz (¾ lb)
410 g	13 oz
440 g	14 oz
470 g	15 oz
500 g	16 oz (1 lb)
750 g	24 oz (1½ lb)
1 kg	30 oz (2 lb)

LIQUID MEASURES

METRIC	*IMPERIAL*
30 ml	1 fluid oz
60 ml	2 fluid oz
100 ml	3 fluid oz
125 ml	4 fluid oz
150 ml	5 fluid oz (¼ pint/1 gill)
190 ml	6 fluid oz
250 ml	8 fluid oz
300 ml	10 fluid oz (½ pint)
500 ml	16 fluid oz
600 ml	20 fluid oz (1 pint)
1000 ml	1¾ pints

CUPS & SPOON MEASURES

METRIC	*IMPERIAL*
1 ml	¼ tsp
2 ml	½ tsp
5 ml	1 tsp
15 ml	1 tbsp
60 ml	¼ cup
125 ml	½ cup
250 ml	1 cup

HELPFUL MEASURES

METRIC	*IMPERIAL*
3 mm	1/8 in
6 mm	¼ in
1 cm	½ in
2 cm	¾ in
2.5 cm	1 in
5 cm	2 in
6 cm	2½ in
8 cm	3 in
10 cm	4 in
13 cm	5 in
15 cm	6 in
18 cm	7 in
20 cm	8 in
23 cm	9 in
25 cm	10 in
28 cm	11 in
30 cm	12 in (1ft)

HOW TO MEASURE

When using the graduated metric measuring cups, it is important to shake the dry ingredients loosely into the required cup. Do not tap the cup on the table, or pack the ingredients into the cup unless otherwise directed. Level top of cup with a knife. When using graduated metric measuring spoons, level top of spoon with a knife. When measuring liquids in the jug, place jug on a flat surface, check for accuracy at eye level.

OVEN TEMPERATURE

These oven temperatures are only a guide. Always check the manufacturer's manual.

	°C (Celsius)	***°F (Fahrenheit)***	***Gas Mark***
Very low	120	250	1
Low	150	300	2
Moderately low	160	325	3
Moderate	180	350	4
Moderately high	190	375	5
High	200	400	6
	230	450	7